explosion ROCKS springfield

RODRIGO TOSCANO

FENCE BOOKS
albany ny

EXPLOSION *ROCKS* SPRINGFIELD

Cover design by Jess Puglisi
Book design by Rebecca Wolff

Published in the United States by Fence Books
Science Library, 320
University at Albany
1400 Washington Avenue, Albany, NY 12222

www.fenceportal.org

This book was printed by Versa Press and distributed by Small Press Distribution
and Consortium Book Sales and Distribution.

Library of Congress Cataloguing in Publication Data
Toscano, Rodrigo [1964–]
Explosion Rocks Springfield/Rodrigo Toscano

Library of Congress Control Number: 2016933756

ISBN 13: 978-0-9864373-4-2

First Edition
10 9 8 7 6 5 4 3 2

CONTENTS

THE FRIDAY EVENING GAS EXPLOSION IN SPRINGFIELD LEVELED A STRIP CLUB NEXT TO A DAY CARE

What is *explosion* to a slab of *drywall*?

What is "drywall," *exactly*?

HEIGH HO!

Why do people *strip*?

What is "day care"? Why "day"?

What is *night* care?

Why daylight why daylight why daylight.

What is "care," *exactly*?

Gas. Wherefrom gas?

Why gas in cylindrical hollows?

Friday, the day *after* Thursday, the day before Saturday, *always*.

How goes gas *in* there? Surging, surging, surging—

In predetermined patterns—for?

Bodily needs *and* discomforts!

THE FRIDAY EVENING GAS EXPLOSION IN SPRINGFIELD LEVELED A STRIP CLUB NEXT TO A DAY CARE

Thank you for relating the gas explosion in Springfield on Friday. And what did gas *do* to a pair of brownstones in the Brooklyn Township of Greenpoint that same night?

In predetermined patterns surging, *did not* level one household of college adjunct professor + labor coordinator next to one household of finance speculator + boutique entrepreneur.

What is "stripping," *precisely*?

What is "care," *approximately*?

HEIGH HO!

How *dry* is drywall?

THE FRIDAY EVENING GAS EXPLOSION IN SPRINGFIELD LEVELED A STRIP CLUB NEXT TO A DAY CARE

No "stripping," *then*

No "day care," *then*

Was Springfield, Springfield, *then*?

Is Springfield, Springfield *now*?

Has Springfield *ever* been Springfield?

What is *im*plosion?

What is *ex*plosion?

HEIGH HO!

What is to *plode*?

THE FRIDAY EVENING GAS EXPLOSION IN SPRINGFIELD LEVELED A STRIP CLUB NEXT TO A DAY CARE

Dry, echoey, *frabba jabba* walls.

How'd we end up with dry, echoey, *frabba jabba* walls?

What ifs "wet dries," absolutely, completely?

Are you sure you want to *strip*, right here, right now?

Yes, I'm taken care of—*in* the daytime.

I'm *day*-cared for, thank you. Perhaps in ten years, I'll watch you

HEIGH HO!

perdepistatiplode

"To simultaneously *im*plode and explode (barest act of plode)"

Tonight, let us *perdepistatiplode*.

Tonight, let's not splatter onto the street in four million pieces.

THE FRIDAY EVENING GAS EXPLOSION IN SPRINGFIELD LEVELED A STRIP CLUB NEXT TO A DAY CARE

The Saturday morning gas explosion in Manhattan leveled an Off-Track Betting Parlor next to a Correctional Facility.

The Sunday midday gas explosion in Manila leveled a U.S. Navy Mess Hall next to an Intergalactic Hyperspace Space Station.

The Monday afternoon gas explosion in San Diego leveled an Intensive Care Unit for Preemies next to a Veterans of War Lodge.

The Tuesday midnight gas explosion in Simplicity, Utah, leveled a Military Surplus Depot next to a *reverse* strip club (outfits fly back to the bods at the *end* of the act) in Complexity, Nevada.

The Wednesday gas explosion at sun-up in Houma, Louisiana, leveled a Crawfish Storage Tank next to a Benzene Superfund Site aloft in an Anti-Gravitation Field.

The Thursday gas explosion at sundown in Rhode Island leveled a Prestigious Arts & Architecture & Poetics school next to a Victorian Presbyterian Chapel made of quarried stone from 200 miles away—that narrow red door is your entry point.

What is *need*?

What is *comfort*?

What does *perdepistatiplode* achieve, *precisely*?

Is drywall *interested*?

At the end of the day, are steel beams better listeners than storefront windows?

Why nighttime why nighttime why nighttime.

THE FRIDAY EVENING GAS EXPLOSION IN SPRINGFIELD LEVELED A STRIP CLUB NEXT TO A DAY CARE

The gas explosion in Springfield on Friday evening spared a day care next to a strip club.

At the beginning of every day, what is to be *spared*?

What is to be *felled*?

HEIGH HO!

At the *end* of the day, are steel buns equal to municipal zoning definitions?

At all times, what is *fire*?

Is fire—on fire—at every moment of—*every* fire?

Give it a break. We're *burning up* here.

Is fire *keen* on "burning"?

Is fire alert?

Is fire hopelessly, beautifully distracted?

Is fire *itself* in the act of stripping?

Or is it fire's thing to make *others* strip?

frabba jabba

In approximate patterns, surging, amassing, escaping—"culture" "planning" "accident" "conciliation" "life"

THE FRIDAY EVENING GAS EXPLOSION IN SPRINGFIELD LEVELED A STRIP CLUB NEXT TO A DAY CARE

"That's what you're telling us, right?"

"Actually, the gas explosion *made* the evening *into* a strip club, which *sprung* Springfield *out of* the Day Care Center that *for the time being* was a form of..."

"—yeah?"

"*frabba jabba*: regulations, municipalities, nation states, civilizations, procreative policing for millennia, fire *and* ritual, thus stripping, though not "stripping" per se, whence *care*, thence"

THE FRIDAY EVENING GAS EXPLOSION IN SPRINGFIELD LEVELED A STRIP CLUB NEXT TO A DAY CARE

What is *leveling* to a bit of stability?

What is "stability," *exactly*?

HEIGH HO!

Why do people *slink*?

What is it to have "slackness," to slink?

What gives "slack" its slickness?

What is *schlook it up slick n' slimy* "care?"

What is "doink," *precisely*?

Croink. Wherefrom Foink?

Why doink in croinky foinkiness?

Priday, the dearth *after* Pursday, the fray before Paturday, *always*.

How goes PSHSHSHSHSHSHSH *in* there?

Escapes

In random patterns—for?

THE FRIDAY EVENING GAS EXPLOSION IN SPRINGFIELD LEVELED A STRIP CLUB NEXT TO A DAY CARE

Club

It's a *strip*

Club

What is PSHSHSHSHSHSHSHSHSHSHSHSHSHSHSHSH more or less?

Is attire approximate, or precise?

Is approximate a form of exactness?

Are violence and care polar opposite forms of Life's governance?

Is stripping an over-intellectualized form of the Death Dance?

Are you *as one*?

Why twilight why twilight why twilight.

THE FRIDAY EVENING GAS EXPLOSION IN SPRINGFIELD LEVELED A STRIP CLUB NEXT TO A DAY CARE

I don't <doink> understand <doink> at all...really...and it's <doink> okay.

THE FRIDAY EVENING GAS EXPLOSION IN SPRINGFIELD LEVELED A STRIP CLUB NEXT TO A DAY CARE.

I don't understand...at all...and it's <doink><doink>—<doink> not <doink><doink>—<doink>—<doink>—<doink> okay, really.

THE FRIDAY EVENING GAS EXPLOSION IN SPRINGFIELD LEVELED A STRIP CLUB NEXT TO A DAY CARE.

I get it, totally. Okay. Wow. In-<doink>—<doink><doink>—<doink> tense.

THE FRIDAY EVENING GAS EXPLOSION IN SPRINGFIELD LEVELED A STRIP CLUB NEXT TO A DAY CARE.

Okay, I get it, totally. Big   <doink>   deal.

THE FRIDAY EVENING GAS EXPLOSION IN SPRINGFIELD LEVELED A STRIP CLUB NEXT TO A DAY CARE

Echoey

Springfield, Massachusetts

Massachusetts, USA

USA, Planet Q

Near miss!

On target!

In the cards

Random Shuffle

Decision Makers

Process Taskers

God Bless The Fuckers *Theirs*

God Bless The Fuckers *Ours*

Pipe Fitters Local 1138

Perdepistatiplosive

THE FRIDAY EVENING GAS EXPLOSION IN SPRINGFIELD LEVELED A STRIP CLUB NEXT TO A DAY CARE

Hm.

THE FRIDAY EVENING GAS EXPLOSION IN SPRINGFIELD LEVELED A STRIP CLUB NEXT TO A DAY CARE

Compañeros, obviamente el peligro presente no fue adequadamente identificado, prioratizado, y, compañeros, no seguido por control del peligro actual; compañeros, todo esto resulto en que la eliminacion del peligro actual no fue posible, compañeros. Compañeros, su atención por favor.

THE FRIDAY EVENING GAS EXPLOSION IN SPRINGFIELD LEVELED A STRIP CLUB NEXT TO A DAY CARE

So you're saying . . .

Doink is *frabba jabba*, but in a decayed state of HEIGH HO!

Foinked by Life?

What is Life—*general frame, please.*

What is Death—*general frame, please.*

How goes doink *in* here—amassing, amassing, amassing—

Essssssssssssscapes

Random lovely—

In volatile patterns—for?

THE FRIDAY EVENING GAS EXPLOSION IN SPRINGFIELD LEVELED A STRIP CLUB NEXT TO A DAY CARE

Explosion to a slab of drywall—is nothing.

Drywall is nothing become *something* on the way to nothing as something.

Because when people strip—the sun comes up.

Radiated Heat of the Plant Kingdom Stored.

In precise patterns delivered.

Sindicat des Travailleurs D'Énergie, Locale 224

Saint-Felecien, Québec

Québec, Le Canada

Le Canada, Planèt Q (Version 2)

Pour plaisirs et désagréments d'organes

THE FRIDAY EVENING GAS EXPLOSION IN SPRINGFIELD LEVELED A STRIP CLUB NEXT TO A DAY CARE

For

To

Lay

Deep

Pipe

"Heigh"

"Ho"

——

As

To

Plode

Per

Pound

Prime

Pumps

——

As

Per

Force

Of

Flow

Fill

Flange

——

For

To

Make

Fire

Flame

Strip

Plode

THE FRIDAY EVENING GAS EXPLOSION IN SPRINGFIELD LEVELED A STRIP CLUB NEXT TO A DAY CARE

Are you *doubly* sure you want to *perdepistatiplode* right here, right *now*?
—There's a <doink>—<doink><doink>—<doink> *frabba jabba*

THE FRIDAY EVENING GAS EXPLOSION IN SPRINGFIELD LEVELED A STRIP CLUB NEXT TO A DAY CARE.

I'm *twighlight* cared for, yes, and it's <doink>—<doink><doink>—<doink> foinky
and <doink> state regulated.

THE FRIDAY EVENING GAS EXPLOSION IN SPRINGFIELD LEVELED A STRIP CLUB NEXT TO A DAY CARE.

In ten minutes, maybe five, any moment really—oop, *here I go*
To be felled <doink><doink>—<doink> to get <doink>—<doink><doink> spared.

THE FRIDAY EVENING GAS EXPLOSION IN SPRINGFIELD LEVELED A STRIP CLUB NEXT TO A DAY CARE

How goes . . .

SHSHSHSHSHSHSHSHSHSHSH p'

SHSHSHSHSHSHSHSHSHSHSH p' p' p' p'

SHSHSHSHSHSHSHSHSHSHSH p' p'

SHSHSHSHSHSHSHSHSHSHSH p'

SHSHSHSHSHSHSHSHSHSHSH p'

in there?

What is it to—"tease"—*focus frame, please.*

What is it—to be—"croinked"—*focus frame, please.*

How goes Life *out* there? Scraping, scratching, scuffling—

Steady unstable—

Plodes

In traceable patterns—for?

Beauty Cake

THE FRIDAY EVENING GAS EXPLOSION IN SPRINGFIELD LEVELED A STRIP CLUB NEXT TO A DAY CARE

In cylindrical hollows—my attention

In cylindrical hollows—my visioning

In cylindrical hollows—my remembrance

In cylindrical hollows—my devotion

In cylindrical hollows—my fear

In cylindrical hollows—my escape

In cylindrical hollows—my discovery

In cylindrical hollows—my occlusion

In cylindrical hollows—my

Perdepistatiplosivity

THE FRIDAY EVENING GAS EXPLOSION IN SPRINGFIELD LEVELED A STRIP CLUB NEXT TO A DAY CARE

"Awright, so let's get this straight. *After* you locked-out / tagged-out the c/o valve, then what?"

"I bled the premise outpoints to harmonize the incoming to optimum."

"You bled the premise outpoints to harmonize the incoming to optimum."

"Yes."

"Were the valve caps sealed to spec?"

"The tag-out said they were."

"Did you log that tag-out?"

"Yes."

"Where's the log kept?"

"Central office."

"What's that 'Beauty Cake' tattoo on your forehead about?"

"It's my way of . . .

Amm (p') *assing*

Amm (p' p' p' p') *assing*

Amm (p' p') *assing*

Amm (p') *assing*"

"It's your way of . . . awright . . . who . . . who, uh . . . who . . ."

———

HEIGH HO!

What is it to *sprit*?

PSHSHSHSHSHSHSH

SHSHSHSHSHSHSH

"Got it, so, before you remove"

"—*toss*"

"Ok, toss the . . . tiara?"

"—*sweet roughie*"

"Sweet roughie, all right, before the sweet roughie is tossed"

"—*as*"

"As?"

"Not 'before'—*as*"

"Got it. *As* the sweet roughie is tossed . . . the baby spoon . . . finds its way into . . .

The laws of four millennia synchronized by an immense gas cloud clock
—at the edge of the galaxy, pumping, thumping, beats."

"*You got it, honey.*"

THE FRIDAY EVENING GAS EXPLOSION IN SPRINGFIELD LEVELED A STRIP CLUB NEXT TO A DAY CARE

Four million pieces of

frabba jabba

As One

Wet

In the downpour of

A conflagration douser's

Cylindrical hollow

Beautifully distracting

Flame

As to

Give comfort to

Daytime & Nighttime

Needs

As to

perdepistatiplode

Comfort

For to

Sprit

Beauty Cake

Buns of steel

Pour la lutte ouvrière

At twilight

Prime

Foink

THE FRIDAY EVENING GAS EXPLOSION IN SPRINGFIELD LEVELED A STRIP CLUB NEXT TO A DAY CARE

Companiers, obvious the peril present identity inadequate, priority-making absence add, companiers, *un*queued to action control potential of peril; *companiers*, resultant, in whole, was elimination none of peril actual therein, *companiers*. *Companiers*, attentions yours, for a favor.

THE FRIDAY EVENING GAS EXPLOSION IN SPRINGFIELD LEVELED A STRIP CLUB NEXT TO A DAY CARE

For mouth, *bouche*
Cock, *bitte*
Ass, *cul*
Cooch, *chatte*
For the head, *tête*

———

All units 4-alarm, code Orange. 278 Hunt @ Harrison
Ah oui, my bitte in your cul in my bouche, ah oui

Copy base. Ladder 6, 3 minutes out
Ah oui, my cul in your cul, in your bouche, ah oui

Copy base. Ladder 12, 2 out
Ah oui my bouche in your *bouche in my cul—in your chatte, ah oui*

Copy base. Ladder 17, on site
Ah oui, your chatte in my bouche in your cul in my *chatte in* your *bouche, ah oui*

Copy base, Ladder 4, we have adjoining 3-alarm on site
Ah oui my bitte, in my bitte, in your cul (in your bouche), AH OUI

Man down! Man down! Ladder 2, code Red, adjoining
Ah oui, your chatte in my bouche in your cul in my bitte (ah oui)

My tête? C'est . . .

Perdepistatiplosif

———

What is need, *by contact*?

What is care, *by contact*?

What is comfort, *by contact*?

What is to have—give—*slack*?

HEIGH HO!

What is it to *slink* daily—in *croink*—by *foink*?

THE FRIDAY EVENING GAS EXPLOSION IN SPRINGFIELD LEVELED A STRIP CLUB NEXT TO A DAY CARE

Drywall—on its back, flat.

Drywall—on its side, horizontal.

Drywall—standing, vertical.

Drywall—side-by-side, flush.

Drywall—capped by ceiling mortar slab.

Drywall—receives a layer of primer gray.

Drywall—accepts a coat of moonless midnight sable.

Drywall—wears a film of sweat, saliva, semen, and commodified cooch nectar —without a contract.

Drywall:

Stoic and Expressive

Conceptual and Lyrical

Engaged and Ascetic

Drywall, about to

Strip

"Frontinus, chief planner *urbis*, at the behest of the Emperor, has seen to it that methane build-up from the *cloaca maxima* (which flows directly beneath the Basilica Julia) is minimized."

"And how?"

"M'lord, from what I am told, an orphanage, that once housed our most worthy Gallic slaves (booty from our forebears' forebears' victories on the plains of the *Po*), was stripped of rock and mortar and made into a pressure-relieving rivulet, one-half league in length, the *cloaca minoris*."

"Marvelous, we must guard against Rome's most spirited, halest bowels, from setting us afire."

"Indeed, my lord."

THE FRIDAY EVENING GAS EXPLOSION IN SPRINGFIELD LEVELED A STRIP CLUB NEXT TO A DAY CARE

Echoey

Gluteus Medius to Rectus Femoris

Rectus Femoris to Piriformis

Piriformis to Adductor Longus

Off-kilter

On the beat

In sequence

Connective patterns

Erotic Taskers

Accounts Adjusters

God Damn The Shiftwork—*theirs*

God Damn The Shiftwork—*ours*

Amalgamated Adult Entertainers

Coiled cobra

AAE, Local 39

Will strike, if provoked

THE FRIDAY EVENING GAS EXPLOSION IN SPRINGFIELD LEVELED A STRIP CLUB NEXT TO A DAY CARE

High value items recovered: deep-soak 20s bathtub with brass-plated lion's feet.

High value items destroyed: matching "Sumerian" toilet.

Other items: Mother Superior habit and wooden cross necklace stuffed into case of 15-year Johnnie Green found in looter's Hyundai Elantra; Warden Wild Willie sequin chemise beneath perp's jumpsuit.

Estimated total value: $680

THE FRIDAY EVENING GAS EXPLOSION IN SPRINGFIELD LEVELED A STRIP CLUB NEXT TO A DAY CARE

Four million pieces of

frabba jabba

Dry

At high noon

In a downpour of

Sun's beams

Wistfully forgetful

Pieces of One

Pulse

Swept up

For to

Take refuge in

Twilight's

Urges

Double bag

Sorrows

At evening

Calmly

As when

Sapiens ("the knower")

Feels it

Eyes of Jewels

Alert

To others'

Wants

As daybreak's

New demands

Seek

Tribute

THE FRIDAY EVENING GAS EXPLOSION IN SPRINGFIELD LEVELED A STRIP CLUB NEXT TO A DAY CARE

Symptoms: chronic boredom, manic arousal

Diagnosis: Care as care might, care cared care to peril, and further imperiled peril—caring more, so much so, that peril cared *only* for peril, imperiling care itself (by then neither caring nor imperiling)

Prognosis: *croinked to the foink*

Treatment: "I love you" "I love *you*"

Prescription: *perdepistatiplosive* (morning, noon, night)

THE FRIDAY EVENING GAS EXPLOSION IN SPRINGFIELD LEVELED A STRIP CLUB NEXT TO A DAY CARE

Springfield bleeding Springfield

Croinkdom

Kish, seat of Sumer
Released

Procession of
As *One*

Horns, Drums, Harps
In precise patterns
Beats pulsing

Arterial valves
Ploding

Bubbled oxygen
Surging

Amassing
Quivering bellies

——

What is it to *lust* City?

What is it to *take* Country?

How goes "heigh" "ho"

Everywhere

At once?

THE FRIDAY EVENING GAS EXPLOSION IN SPRINGFIELD LEVELED A STRIP CLUB NEXT TO A DAY CARE

"*This* 'Barter Pie' tattoo?

It's for the 'discerning'

Flashed while in Cat Crawl

After the Eyes of Jewels

Before the Limb Tossing

As the lyric settles

Siphoning up the beat

'Is fire, fire?' 'Is fire, fire?'

Love it, because by then

Discerning gentlefolk

Are *inside* the ductwork

Soshies—prate on 'concern'

Cappies—straight up applaud

We just say, *sapienized*

Meaning Mother's Keepsakes

Cloaking *frabba jabba*

Set to plode left or right

So that's how I girl *up*

Every night to make this

Amm (p' p' p') *assing*

—escape . . .

My *real* name is Lulu Chateau, *yes*

I publish poems.

No, I've never heard of you."

THE FRIDAY EVENING GAS EXPLOSION IN SPRINGFIELD LEVELED A STRIP CLUB NEXT TO A DAY CARE

The Juptiterian midday lead effusion on Ganymede liquefied a zinc bed next to a crater rim.

The Uranian morning argon ionization on Oberon dispersed a helium cloud next to an ammonium pool.

The Neptunian magnetosphere at dusk on Triton catalyzed carbon dioxide to glow red next to a haze of methane blue.

The Saturnian midnight hydrogen fission at the core vaporized iron sludge next to a vent of nucleated nickel.

The Mercurian afternoon potassium excretion at the crust sucked sodium into a xenon vacuole next to a krypton spouter cone.

The Martian nitrogen de-misting at daybreak in the Mare Erythraeum made visible a silicon chunklet next to a silicon chunklet.

The Venusian early evening volcanic updrafts into the troposphere rained down sulfur clods into a neon whirlpool next to the *Venera 8* wreckage heap.

THE FRIDAY EVENING GAS EXPLOSION IN SPRINGFIELD LEVELED A STRIP CLUB NEXT TO A DAY CARE

"The Liberty Box checked to spec as did the Libidinal Lines at the Thought Crossers.

Strange thing was the Gonad Gauge didn't register the Need Switches.

Good thing the Big O Override tripped the Care Breakers right then.

I'm sure that's what kicked in the Ego Ventilator, eventually firing up a Poetic Alarm.

. . . .

'The Locked Out / Tagged Out American'—that's the working title.

Sure, soon as this draft is *stabilized*, I'll pop it to you.

Oh, one more thing, the Personal Protection Equipment locker was found to be broken into, but no one's been seen wearing the distinctive yellow hi-res Baby Doll Nightie."

THE FRIDAY EVENING GAS EXPLOSION IN SPRINGFIELD LEVELED A STRIP CLUB NEXT TO A DAY CARE

What is *blood* to constrictive tissue?

What is "constriction," *exactly*?

HEIGH HO!

Why do people Nation Idol Gorge?

What is "engorgement"? Why "gorge"?

What is *disen*gorgement?

Why vascularity, why mascularity, why femascularity?

What is Nation Idol Gorge, *precisely*?

Flame. Wherefrom flame?

Why flame in both nostrils, ploding?

Friday, the day *within* Friday, the day within *within* Friday, *always*.

How goes flame *in* here? Spittletatootling, spittletatootling, spittletatootling—

In gaugeable patterns—for?

Regulated flow—and

frabba jabba

THE FRIDAY EVENING GAS EXPLOSION IN SPRINGFIELD LEVELED A STRIP CLUB NEXT TO A DAY CARE

"*Thank you*. I wear it, strong.

The print fits, don't it?

And *foink*'s all over it.

As the event recedes

It's *echoey*, this word

But here's a stage for it

And the head space for it

Shit, *nobody* noticed

Nobody *popped* from there

Blown off—for *takes*—that word

Somebody—yeah, *could* have

Strutted—tall, called forth—far

So I do, *echoey*

And the word and me, well

We work *in* the ears, deep

Make what's seen—seem to be

'Evening gas explosion'

Stone cold bitch—phrase, leashing

'Leveled-a-strip-club-next-to-a-day-care'

But the *word*—slinks between

'Evening' 'gas' 'explosion'

Unseen—for all to see

Unheard—for all to hear

Heat pressed onto this blouse

I wear it, strong, all day

It's *perplexing*—and bright!"

THE FRIDAY EVENING GAS EXPLOSION IN SPRINGFIELD LEVELED A STRIP CLUB NEXT TO A DAY CARE

"The equinox midday dolmen collapse in Cambria flattened a wizard's wicker tent next to a pigpen."

Project Abstract
The final phase of the Paleolithic period in Cambria brought about radical transformations in the conception of the X-Hole. The emerging beaker artisanal class, having failed to "steal the seed" from the reindeer warrior strata, turned to elaborate rituals that signaled the demise of both contending classes. This project aims to prove the seed was in fact, acquired—then lost, found again, and lost again.

Project Timeline
Phase 1: Acquisition of earthmoving equipment
Phase 2: Acquisition of local casual labor
Phase 3: Sift, collect, identify, interpret
Phase 4: Produce report for G.A.P.S. database

Staff Bios
Jill Quill, MFA Poetry, cupcake shop manager.
Joe Blow, MFA Fiction, cupcake shop associate.
Jen Jiffy, MFA Nonfiction, cupcake shop trainee.

Amount Requested: $754, 000

THE FRIDAY EVENING GAS EXPLOSION IN SPRINGFIELD LEVELED A STRIP CLUB NEXT TO A DAY CARE

Porcelain chips . . .

Rubber toilet float, rolling east . . .

Last night's imminence, elsewhere . . .

Bits, shards, scraps, charred . . .

Spartacus sprinklers . . .

"I hate writers who *self jack*" . . .

Midday sun—coursing west . . .

Shards—sensational . . .

Scraps—overwhelming . . .

Bits—demure, seductive . . .

"I hate writers who *self jack*" . . .

Silica runoff sludge puddle . . .

Polyvinyl off-gassing—*ellipses* . . .

Springfield, poking about, peeking in . . .

Log it—

Perdepistatiplosive

All around

THE FRIDAY EVENING GAS EXPLOSION IN SPRINGFIELD LEVELED A STRIP CLUB NEXT TO A DAY CARE

That's next to a house of worship, next to The House of Pets, next to a firehouse, next to an ale house, next to a house of comfort, next to the Historical Preservation Society's Poets House, next to Bob's House of Finance, next to the House of Costumes, next to reclamation project housing, next to a meth house, next to a safe house, next to the House of Hope, next to the House of Action, next to the House of High Minded Adult Naughtiness, next to a gas pipeline distribution hub, next to Pipe Fitters Local 1138, next to a cupcake shop.

THE FRIDAY EVENING GAS EXPLOSION IN SPRINGFIELD LEVELED A STRIP CLUB NEXT TO A DAY CARE

Chorus: *"Jank"*

This brand of cupcake mix?
—*Jank*

This velcro snap garter belt?
—*Jank*

This old control panel?
—*Jank*

This new contract?
—*Jank*

This strategy session?
—*Jank*

This form of prayer?
—*Jank*

This place of operation?
—*Jank*

This dope right here?
—*Jank*

This title deed?
—*Jank*

This Bullwinkle rave hat?
—*Jank*

This investment's vistas?
—*Jank*

This venerated pauper's versifications?
—*Jank*

This style of comfort?
—*Jank*

This Crooked Rooster IPA?
—*Jank*

This fire station eurotrance party?
—*Jank*

This hamster Ferris wheel with blinking lights?
—*Jank*

This pastor's elevator metaphors?
—*Jank*

This kind of care?
—*Jank*

This way of stripping?
—*Jank*

This town right here—serious?
—*Jank*

This evening, and all evenings before it, and after, forevermore?
—*Jank*

THE FRIDAY EVENING GAS EXPLOSION IN SPRINGFIELD LEVELED A STRIP CLUB NEXT TO A DAY CARE

I remember the breeze right before . . .
Burs of—was it willow—slant-falling.
The gray sidewalk, schist granules, scattering.
A brown dumpster lid smushing its green plastic sandwich meat.
A rat made its debut, but for a moment.

I remember an awning string's knotted tip soft-thudding a windowpane
—tympani's uneven beat.
The rustle of stray trash—bass strings, almost rising
—but never.
And the chopper, the chopper—spittletatootling, spittletatootling—
A proud boot landing on obedient asphalt.
The stern uncrying chrome.
The flighty-flames decorative gas tank.

I can't forget the beryllium blue sunshades
—orange hued at a glance.
And the Stars & Bars starched pressed bandana.
Nation Idol Gorge
But for a moment
Then
Boom.

THE FRIDAY EVENING GAS EXPLOSION IN SPRINGFIELD LEVELED A STRIP CLUB NEXT TO A DAY CARE

This child lines up for milk—when—it's time.

That one follows.

This one looks on.

That other one looks to the one looking on.

They both—at the same time—join the line.

There's a tussle for who's first—for 3rd—position.

The rest follow in random patterns, amassing.

The line curves around the little furniture, tubular.

(These heat valves are trusty.

This room is always toasty.)

The line steadily shrinks, child by child

Piling onto the carpet, precisely.

By 6, the center is empty.

By 7, the warriors are lining up next-door, antler by antler, brain by brain.

By 8, twelve disco balls rotate like forty moons around the undiscovered planet "Q".

THE FRIDAY EVENING GAS EXPLOSION IN SPRINGFIELD LEVELED A STRIP CLUB NEXT TO A DAY CARE

"PAAWK! Somewhe' else—you *moron*. This ain't Chiner."

"You—fuck you! Gwei-lo, white devil motherfucker!"

"Yeah? Up yaws!"

"Springfield *suck shit*. You family strip for dolla' food."

"Up yaws, commie bastuhd, move that caw"

"I call Sumerian crew your ass!"

"Move it"

"Sumerian crew shave you man tit"

"What the fawk you tawkin' about?"

"Sumerian crew make you fuck chicken nugget. Springfield *suck*."

"Love it or leave it, moron."

"This my parking prace, Blianna – best stripper give to me"

"I've been hittin' this joint – 10 *yeas*! Brianna—rookie! You—moron!"

"*Who you like* . . . gwei-lo *motherfucker*!"

Spartacus sprinklers (top rail)
Serial no. 21809A
Inspector 480F
Jiangxi Quality Products
Night Hawk Importers, San Bruno, CA
Roman Roads Distributors, Phoenix, AZ
Port of entry, Tacoma, WA
Tankard 10179.03
Inspector 4201
ILO quarterly report:
Case study 1142
Tingting Liu, 23, female
I.D. 41732
Platform 12, line 8, station 4
Muscular skeletal paralysis
3rd metatarsal taped to 2nd   phalangeal
4th proximal splinted to 5th distal
OSHA Region 1 final report:
Incident 2267, explosion (gas)
Inspector 505F
Sprinklers inoperable
Logic Tree branch 20
System of Safety failure
Mitigation device
16 drill holes stoppered
Weld burrs not filed
Citation: 29CFR.1910.159(c)(12)
Notes: inspector 505F on leave
DOL budget sequestered

PUB.L. 112-25
District 2, 112th Congress
United States of America

THE FRIDAY EVENING GAS EXPLOSION IN SPRINGFIELD LEVELED A STRIP CLUB NEXT TO A DAY CARE

"Is water always wet?

See, I don't believe so.

For sure, I would have been

A tough pre-Socratic.

Water's dry—*all* the time!

The concept of 'sometimes'

Turns everything to crumbs.

We're all raised on 'sometimes'

Keeps us in check, in line.

Water is—*never* wet.

Else, how does it douse fire?

Fire is wet—always.

'Sometimes'—plays no role there.

Some people want *epics*.

Some eat beach sand for lunch.

And what is the result?

Collared—by speech—like this:

'It's like, the like, fire, like,

It was all like, *fiery*,

Like I'm all, like, that's like,

Fiery, that fire, like I

Know, but like—I'm all like . . . '

See? The very *approach*

To all phenomena

Felled—at the point of birth.

The *matter*, is rather:

What is—water—to fire?

What is *fire*—to water?

These questions have straight backs

These questions bear fresh fruit.

No? Mouth it for yourself:

'Fire is . . . *sometimes* dry'

'Water is . . . *sometimes* wet'

Ugh!"

THE FRIDAY EVENING GAS EXPLOSION IN SPRINGFIELD LEVELED A STRIP CLUB NEXT TO A DAY CARE

That Friday evening, the Russian consulate served:

Nuts-and-Bolts Soup
Copper Mesh Wire Salad
Cutlets of Vanadium Reinforced Steel
Two sides of Chromium Rivets (one galvanized, one magnetized)

Uncorked was *Premium 100 Million Year Liquid Gas.*

The contained-cheery German robot raised a goblet in a toast, followed by the Turk, Romanian, Hungarian, and the shy, slim Canadian robot leaning against the fireplace.

"To President Putin,

This era of poetry,

And to all of our medium-sized cities

Their version of traditional and/or avant-garde sexualities."

THE FRIDAY EVENING GAS EXPLOSION IN SPRINGFIELD LEVELED A STRIP CLUB NEXT TO A DAY CARE

What is *compulsion* to a sliver of *free will*?

What is "free will" *exactly*?

HEIGH HO!

Why do people *jack*?

What is "cosmic trust"? Why "cosmic"?

What is the *Planet Q Plan*?

Why 1st shift why 2nd why 3rd why 4th why 5th.

What is "jack," *approximately*?

Ovule, wherefrom ovule?

Why spermatozoa on diamond-coated superhighways?

Thursday, bashing into Friday, Friday, bashing into Saturday, *always*.

How goes "sapiens" *up in* there? Flaking, sliming, frothing—

In regulated patterns—for?

Postcards from Springfield—*and*

Beauty Cake Frozen Bar Wrappers.

THE FRIDAY EVENING GAS EXPLOSION IN SPRINGFIELD LEVELED A STRIP CLUB NEXT TO A DAY CARE

"Bleed it here, the gas—watch.

Gauge zero's—see, both ends.

Cinch it—there, till it pools.

Gauge should read 25.

Double tap it, why not.

Eight, has to be eight feet

O2 tanks and this one

Or five foot wall between.

Now, that's premise regs, right?

C.O.'s have their *own* regs.

Zone, each one has its reg.

Same principal, you'll see.

Double strap it, always.

These trucks, they shake, awful.

Brewskies at The Bouillon?

Nah. Stick a fork in me

This shift always, I'm cooked.

Thursday—right, at the hall.

You should chair it, why not?

All right, buddy, be safe.

Don't let them gals fleece ya."

THE FRIDAY EVENING GAS EXPLOSION IN SPRINGFIELD LEVELED A STRIP CLUB NEXT TO A DAY CARE

"Unbutton here, this strap.

Even jugs, see, real nice.

Now clip on this red tail

One minute into it.

Double flare it, why not.

Five, can only be five

Per booth—including you.

Or eight, if two of you.

Now, that's this club's reg, right?

Other clubs make their own.

Boss, each has a "vision."

Same old dance, count on it.

Well, maybe two buttons.

These strobes, they blind, crazy.

Night owl shots at The Coop?

Nah. Scoop me on a cone

This shift always, I'm licked.

Thursday—right, at my house.

You should chair it, why not?

All right, honey, be safe.

Don't let them guys steer ya."

THE FRIDAY EVENING GAS EXPLOSION IN SPRINGFIELD LEVELED A STRIP CLUB NEXT TO A DAY CARE

"Spread out the ice like this.

Twelve chocolate, three white milks.

Watch how I wedge them in.

Roster should say fifteen.

Do a roll call, why not.

Four, only four can go

This bathroom and that one.

That's *this* center's regs, right?

Other ones have their own.

Counties, each one decides.

Similar norms, you'll see.

Yeah, check for leaky ones

These cartons, they rip, tons.

Rump shake shooters at Ski's?

Nah. Crunk on without me

This shift always, I'm zonked.

Thursday—right, at the rec.

You should chair it, why not?

All right then girl, be safe.

Don't let these kids crank you."

THE FRIDAY EVENING GAS EXPLOSION IN SPRINGFIELD LEVELED A STRIP CLUB NEXT TO A DAY CARE

Fracked—your sense of choice

Fracked—your choice of choice

Fracked—your choice's choice

Fracked—your choice's choice's choice

In cylindrical hollows—the idea

In cylindrical hollows—the application

In cylindrical hollows—the conversion

In cylindrical hollows—the freedom

Twilight care—when you don't

Twilight care—when you can't

Twilight care—when you won't

Twilight care—when you most definitely certainly ought not to

Frabba jabba—because the prime minister said so

Frabba jabba—because the secretary of state said so

Frabba jabba—because the president's press secretary said so

Frabba jabba—because Sargon, Lord of Sumer's punctured bronze mask seems to say so

THE FRIDAY EVENING GAS EXPLOSION IN SPRINGFIELD LEVELED A STRIP CLUB NEXT TO A DAY CARE

I remember the plume right after . . .
Orbs of—was it cinnamon—black-rising.
Vapor gray whitening shingle powder rain.
A dumpster lid sheared off a gravestone's angel face.
A hawk's claws claimed the stump.

I remember two spouts of thin flame, blue, making an X
—mind's waking dream.
The hissing of gurgling plastic, supplicant—sick
—stomach's inner eyeball.
And the bathtub, the bathtub—sittin' pretty—sittin' pretty—
The hysteric roof flopping on an unfazed floor.
The wise, ever-wakeful steel beams.
The cheery glass—beaming—everywhere.

I can't forget that purple doorknob
—horny at a glance.
And the plump couch stuffing foam, blazing, angry.
City's Final Chorus
But for a moment
Then
Shhh.

THE FRIDAY EVENING GAS EXPLOSION IN SPRINGFIELD LEVELED A STRIP CLUB NEXT TO A DAY CARE

The Saturday evening crawfish boil in Mandeville, LA, made frisky four revelers side by side in a hot tub.

The gas storm 1,000 feet below warped the shale bed to a 2.5 rattler on the Richter.

Enough to leak poetry 1,298 miles away?

The Sunday evening jet's vapor trail over Brooklyn garlanded a witch's breasts with a bison tooth,

Dangling.

THE FRIDAY EVENING GAS EXPLOSION IN SPRINGFIELD LEVELED A STRIP CLUB NEXT TO A DAY CARE

"The Opportunity Button calibration was up to date as was the Back Up Situation Circuit.

Good thing was the Deep Doubt Meter powered up the Trust Effusion Chamber.

Even better, the *Secondary* Input Charge overrode the Primary Breakers just then.

I'm sure that's what restarted the Speculation Fans, eventually cooling down the Main Frazzle Unit.

. . . .

'The Lucky-Fated Americans'—that's the new working title.

Sure, as soon as this draft is *stabilized*, I'll pop it to you.

Oh, one more thing, the Cosmic Transport Wormholes have since closed up, but one is sure to open up soon, especially if you commit to this Invisible Pink Leopard Print Full Body Suit in a pitch dark closet, the sun directly overhead."

THE FRIDAY EVENING GAS EXPLOSION IN SPRINGFIELD LEVELED A STRIP CLUB NEXT TO A DAY CARE

"Is fire always flaming?

See, I think not always.

You bet, I'm a full on

Phenomenologist.

Rarely—is fire flamed up.

The concept of 'always'

Douses audacity.

We suckle it like babes,

Keeps us from forging out.

Fire—*rarely* fires all up.

Else, how's the flame preserved?

Fire—is a shy actor.

'Always'—has no play there.

Some spectators want thrills

Some jump naked through hoops.

And where does that leave us?

Caged—by gestures—like this:

'The smoke, um, it, it just.

Um, well, wait, um, it, *well*.

I think, is *that*, um, wait.

Hm, is, um, *this*, um, wait.

Did, um, it, just, well, *hmm*.'

See? The very *desire*

For all phenomena

Eternally blunted.

The *pith*—should rather be:

What is fire—to flaming?

What is *flame*—firing up?

These concerns have strong guts.

These concerns bolster life.

No? Try *this* on for size:

'Flame is . . . *always* fired up'

'Fire is . . . *always* flaming'

Terrible!"

THE FRIDAY EVENING GAS EXPLOSION IN SPRINGFIELD LEVELED A STRIP CLUB NEXT TO A DAY CARE

X-bot—could have—*RUN*—to the spot—had it "the power."

X-bot—could have—*DRIVEN* there—had it "the means to."

X-bot—could have—*WALKED*—had it been "ready to."

X-bot—could have *FLOWN* there—had it—*communicated* with X-bots—to do—*just that*.

——

1st Tale of the X-Bot
Emergency Rescue Plan A

"Stand here!"
"Stand there!"

2nd Tale of the X-Bot
Emergency Rescue Plan B

"Crouch here!"
"Crawl there!"

3rd Tale of the X-Bot
Emergency Rescue Plan C

"Step there!"
"Stop here!"

——

X-Bot—had it:

Courage
Tenacity
Ambition
Wits
Passion

A tad more
X Sexy Botness

In a pinch

THE FRIDAY EVENING GAS EXPLOSION IN SPRINGFIELD LEVELED A STRIP CLUB NEXT TO A DAY CARE

I don't remember the very moment . . .
Flashes of—was I daydreaming—Biloxi Bound.
The termite swarm at dusk, balling up, sprinkling.
A skeeter swirling in its hotel pool—for the first time.
A no-see-um bug popped out from nowhere—but for a moment—to romp.

I can't say I recall Cleopatra's hairpiece flying off in a speeding four-cylinder vehicle
—Empire of the Great Somewhere, but never.
And the flying fish, the flying fish—hither-flopping, hither-flopping—
The carefree palms, twerking, injured.
The bald, unyielding sun, giddy.
Tentative feet in knee-high water, gripping.

Have I forgotten the name of that triple IPA—something like
—*Rondez the Moon à la Batshit*.
And the ample sized black pockadots—in my eyes, twerking, carefully.
Empire of the Great Somewhere
But for a moment
Then
Then

THE FRIDAY EVENING GAS EXPLOSION IN SPRINGFIELD LEVELED A STRIP CLUB NEXT TO A DAY CARE

She wishes she could weave words in space made of each letter's squiggly string.

For instance, FRIDAY, its F lancing its stem below, mooring it down sturdy while pulling up F's horizontal top bar till it points straight upwards, and stretching it, as it thins out in the distance, super fine string to loop around R's trunk a hundred times, tightening a knot around R's curve, leaving a snug hole to pull I's dot into it, I's trunk now alone, from both ends, she loops it around D, so that D is in a perfect circle—pleasing, but it's disturbing, the A and Y now outside the circle, she weaves them together in space (their own space), creating an illusion of X, illusion of X is her refuge now, also her rock throwing promontory

from *inside* FRIDAY

in Springfield.

THE FRIDAY EVENING GAS EXPLOSION IN SPRINGFIELD LEVELED A STRIP CLUB NEXT TO A DAY CARE

The *love implosion* in New Orleans on Sunday Morning gave rise to a twilight care next to a mausoleum.

At the beginning of every hour, what is to be *conjured*?

What is to be *spell-struck*?

HEIGH HO!

At the *end* of every year, are weary eyes equal to Standard Computer Screen Definitions?

At all times, what is *vision*?

Is vision—visionary—at every moment of—*every* vision?

Give it a rest. We're *booked up* here.

Is vision bent on betting?

Is vision in-house?

Is vision helplessly, goofily entranced?

Is vision *itself* in the act of guessing?

Or is it vision's thing to make *others* blind?

frabba jabba

In preternatural patterns, flickering, flashing, floating—"The Arts" "Sciences" "Politics" "Humanities" "Death"

THE FRIDAY EVENING GAS EXPLOSION IN SPRINGFIELD LEVELED A STRIP CLUB NEXT TO A DAY CARE

The Monday morning piano dumping into Lake Pontchartrain infuriated an 8-year-old master rhetorician next to a soft-spoken insomniac mother.

A low-pressure system 500 miles east of Honduras generously invited warm air into its lair.

Enough to cycle poetry relentlessly northwest by northeast?

The Tuesday midday eye of the storm over Brooklyn rendered every sound as of a singular piece of music

About to start.

—

Something about . . .

"Cohesion" "Combustion"

Care

THE FRIDAY EVENING GAS EXPLOSION IN SPRINGFIELD LEVELED A STRIP CLUB NEXT TO A DAY CARE

The Wednesday evening methane bed cargo on a barge from Brooklyn to Pleasant Point remained calm next to three excited seagulls.

A ten-foot wall of water 300 by 300 miles politely glided under the barge.

Enough to lift poetry out of its urban slumber?

The Thursday morning pre-conversion tanks in Newtown Creek buckled under 2,000 lbs. per square inch of

The Aesthetics of Repurposing.

——

Something about . . .

"Amnesia" "Compression"

Stripping

THE FRIDAY EVENING GAS EXPLOSION IN SPRINGFIELD LEVELED A STRIP CLUB NEXT TO A DAY CARE

I am saying

Doink—is *frabba jabba*

In a decayed state of "heigh ho"

Foinked—by Life.

What is Life? *Black Bayou Water*

What is Death? *Black Bayou Water*

How goes doink *in* there?

Brewing, brewing, brewing—

Bubbles up—

Random lusty—

In roiling patterns—for?

The Barter Pie Tattoo Parlor in Springfield, Massachusetts.

X-bot—rolled up to the spot.

X-bot—performed what was taught.

X-bot—applied what it's got.

X-bot—content with its lot.

——

Soliloquy of the X-bot

"I can lift off—*here*,
Or I can launch from—*there*."

"I can land—*there*,
Or I can hover—*here*."

"I can batter ram—*hereabouts*,
Or I can tunnel through—*thereabouts*."

"I can—"

——

Thunderous applause.

Sapiens—onlookers, redeemed

For what they had dreamed.

X-bot—victorious

Amid ash, rubble, fumes.

He wishes he could weld words together in space made of each letter's sheared
I-beams.

For instance, EXPLOSION, its E, blasting off its top bar, flash-fusing it to Xs
midpoint, the two creating a "nook" for P to collapse into, then spot-fusing P's
post to E-X, so that L—now off-kilter, follows, falls *into* that flash-arced threesome,
freeing O—to be its super fabulous O-self, but, having to make more supple O's
headstrong tensility by liquefying S, so that thousands of hot drops on the surface
of O—quells the excess, leaving I—now an issue (always an issue) to infix on its most
proximal playmate, a *second* O, teetering on the heap, in lurching anticipation,
having magnetized N's N-ness, requiring an improvised arc flash to cleave the two

atop the sculpture EXPLOSION

in Springfield.

THE FRIDAY EVENING GAS EXPLOSION IN SPRINGFIELD LEVELED A STRIP CLUB NEXT TO A DAY CARE

This child makes an image of the central power station.

That one imitates the detail—in chalk.

This one cups chalk dust in its hands.

That other one blows images into its face.

The four vacate the drawing corner at 2 minutes to noon, exactly.

There's a scramble for who's the next 1st, 2nd, 3rd, and 4th—in the corner.

The rest look on, anxiously.

The bunch looks like supplicants at the gates of purgatory.

(These fluorescents are very efficient.

125 watts is quite sufficient.)

The bunch breaks up, suddenly.

They seek their desks, precisely.

By 6, the center is empty.

By 7, the central station lowers the output, volt by volt, fancy by fancy.

By 8, the town glimpsed from 35, 000 ft. shimmers a $49 purple blouse with sparklers, *intelligence*.

THE FRIDAY EVENING GAS EXPLOSION IN SPRINGFIELD LEVELED A STRIP CLUB NEXT TO A DAY CARE

FACE   THE   BAR

POON   JACK

DON'T   MATTER

ALL'S   ASH

THE FRIDAY EVENING GAS EXPLOSION IN SPRINGFIELD LEVELED A STRIP CLUB NEXT TO A DAY CARE

"'Lips among the Living'

That's the title of it

Or what it was at least.

In the V.I.P. room

Hung high, lorded over

Did its thing, never flinched.

All charred, but if you look

Still, the gargoyles stare out

Some folks—freaked the frick out.

What it was, was a *pain*

A silent scream—reached deep

The moment the door closed.

Now look at it, crumpled

Can't quite make out its *soul*

Fifty Cocked Female Hawk

From its beak, flung towards us

A sort of sausage links

Rope, made of human lips.

Life, it cradled some Life.

The place was otherwise

Pure machine for product

All emotions packaged

Cube after cube after—

Guess, I *will* take it— home."

Spartacus Sprinklers (top rail)
Serial no. 21809A
Scrap metal yard F-2
Stripped steel tankard 28
Sampson Recyclers Ltd., Pittsfield, MA
Steelworkers local 4-12026
Smelting furnace 48
Slab beam rollout batch 81.2014
Semper Fortis Steel Precision Corp, Brooklyn, NY
Steelworkers local 4-200
Section cutting station no. 12
Steel cylinder hollow type 2b
Store & send department 4
Spirit of 76 Commercial Furnishing Corp, Slidell, LA
Steelworkers local 3-275
Sargon Sprinklers (bottom rail)
Serial no. 321911B
Sink coating station 12
Sanding unit 25
Seal testing station no. 7
Sprinklers standard specification 29CFR1910.159(b)
Station inspector 13
Sales packaging room H
Sort and storage garage 4
Second incidence of forklift crushing worker's toes
Spirit of 76 Personnel Motivation Free Cupcake Fridays director, Chet Baker
Steelworkers local 3-275 chief steward, Marynella Fernandez
Section 5, clause 2 "Management shall comply with all state and federal standards"
Safety committee grievance no. 78: unannounced station rotations / inadequate training
Staff training regulation arbitration hearing 501.P.36
Sargon Sprinklers 1st annual wet T-shirt contest
Super Sonic Dance Club, 3rd Floor, Picayune, MS

THE FRIDAY EVENING GAS EXPLOSION IN SPRINGFIELD LEVELED A STRIP CLUB NEXT TO A DAY CARE

"Does smoke often billow?

Be real! Of course it does.

You're quite the philosophe.

Me? I'm more a mover.

Quite often—smoke billows.

The concept of 'rarely'

Makes murky what happens.

We abuse it, a crutch

Knocks out our bust-a-move.

Smoke—is *all* billowing.

Else, how you take on smoke?

Smoke—is a tricky cat.

'Rarely'—can't get with that.

Some dudes here all *timeout*

Some all just suck whistle.

And how does that do us?

Punked—by language—like this:

'Those billows, I'm sorry

Not quite official yet,

And smoke, being registered

As *semi*-official:

Billows can't play with smoke.'

See? The very *whiff* of

Matched teams competition

Gets shut out the picture.

The *shit*—should rather go:

What is smoke—to billows?

How do billows juke smoke?

These inquiries bring game.

These inquiries punch home.

Don't think so? Check *this* out:

'Smoke . . . *rarely*'s billowing'

'Billows . . . *rarely* mean smoke'

Bump that!"

THE FRIDAY EVENING GAS EXPLOSION IN SPRINGFIELD LEVELED A STRIP CLUB NEXT TO A DAY CARE

X-bots

Extend brims, lower brooms—

Fleet ready . . . *cruise* . . . .stop.

One eighty.

X-bots

Open spigots, release foam—

Fleet ready . . . *cruise* . . . stop.

One eighty.

X-bots

Flip vents, activate vacuums—

Fleet ready . . . *cruise* . . . stop.

X-bots

Lock wheels, power down—

Y-bots

Transport X-bots to

Courage Station

Y-bots

Secure X-bots in

Courage Station

Z-bots

Initiate Planet Q Sequence SB-101:

d'doink doink—*cause you do*

d'doink doink—*cause you done did*

d'doink doink—*cause you're gonna done did do*

d'doink doink—*do do do*

THE FRIDAY EVENING GAS EXPLOSION IN SPRINGFIELD LEVELED A STRIP CLUB NEXT TO A DAY CARE

Porcelain shards

Tenderly

Gash plastic bags

Silica dust droplets

Bashfully

Queue up

Rubber toilet float

Gaily

Oops out

Couch-stuffing cinders

Friskily

Fly away

THE FRIDAY EVENING GAS EXPLOSION IN SPRINGFIELD LEVELED A STRIP CLUB NEXT TO A DAY CARE

The gallery, Torsion Test, where the club once stood, has fallen on tough times.

Tough times—is a hard cushion to flop onto.

No matter though, the "Jelly King" (what people call this curator, unbeknownst to the King) is fast at work shoring up his largely uneventful life with a show of his own.

"A show of nothing" he's calling it, preempting the real possibility that no one at all will show up; the King, having comfily settled into this quivering, semi-solid reality.

What the King doesn't know, however, is that this *stuff* holding it all together is:

Class "B" flammable shit.

———

What doesn't *explode* in Springfield

Slowly burns

THE FRIDAY EVENING GAS EXPLOSION IN SPRINGFIELD LEVELED A STRIP CLUB NEXT TO A DAY CARE

Before the club was erected, a general store's foundations were cleared away.

That old store—in limited quantities—offered:

"Territory Boys" white hemp britches

"Wampum Girl" black sheepskin pantaloons

"Happy Hogan" family size jackrabbit jerky

"Frabba Jabba" beans—by the bushel

From a barrel, Mrs. Barton ladled whisky for the weary.

Midday cups were raised in a toast to the commons:

"For the high sun—*splash*!"

"For the May fly—*zap*!"

"For all good manners—*oooooh—wah*!"

For 42 years and 5 days, folks smoked cigars in the hickory wood aisles—without incident.

In one infernal hour and 23 minutes, Mr. Barton was forced to abstain from musing on stripping down when greeting out of town strangers.

———

"Sargon, Lord of Sumer—like you and me
A stranger to himself, eternally"

THE FRIDAY EVENING GAS EXPLOSION IN SPRINGFIELD LEVELED A STRIP CLUB NEXT TO A DAY CARE

"A polygraph machine in a box of briefs marked 'slightly imperfect'

—that's the last thing we itemized.

The first person we spoke to was the parking lot attendant, 'Shangigo'

—not exactly stock issue, this guy.

When asked about the gas—if there was a smell

—said he *heard* what he saw first, which was nothing,

but that the nothing prompted him to

cross-compare archaic languages on the subjects of sewage treatment and

compensation scales for scribes and slave entertainers

—Shangigo"

"All right, find this guy—bring him in, let's make him talk T-shirts

especially that "*perdepistatiplosive*"

—that one, there's something there (I know it)"

THE FRIDAY EVENING GAS EXPLOSION IN SPRINGFIELD LEVELED A STRIP CLUB NEXT TO A DAY CARE

Bends, male and female, 90°
Bend, male, 45°
Bend, female, 45°

Street elbows, 45°, banded
Side outlet elbows, 45°, non-banded

Tees plain, equal, 90°
Crosses, plain, equal, 90°

Concentric reducing, with threads
Conical joint iron to iron seat
Union, flat seat, without gasket
Conical joint brass to iron seat

Plugs beaded, plugs plain, backnuts

Sockets, plugs, caps, flanges, grip rings, bushings

Injector (pilot and main), couplings

Gate valve, control valve, plug valve, relief valve, hand-powered valve, power valve,
3-way plug valve, 4-way valve

Gauge valve (here)

Bleeder valve (there)

THE FRIDAY EVENING GAS EXPLOSION IN SPRINGFIELD LEVELED A STRIP CLUB NEXT TO A DAY CARE

What is *fantasticality* to a neuron of *gray matter*?

What is "gray matter" *exactly*?

HEIGH HO!

Why do mitochondria *insist*?

What is "death dodge"? Why "dodge"?

What is—*un*-dodge?

Why quasars why quasars why quasars?

What is it to—"quase out" *exactly*?

Plasma. Wherefrom plasma?

Why plasma in cylindrical hollows?

Friday, a light-year after Thursday, the tetra millisecond before Saturday.

How goes d'doink doink *in* here? Squirming, squirming, squirming—

In quantum jittery patterns—for?

Cosmic potential—*and*—actualization!

Books by Rodrigo Toscano

DECK OF DEEDS

COLLAPSIBLE POETICS THEATER

TO LEVELING SWERVE

PLATFORM

PARTISANS

THE DISPARITIES